Ghaby's Organic Garden

by Milesh Jain

Special thanks to:

Beth Martinelli, the awesome editor

Joe Nelson, the fantastic creative illustrator and book designer

Tiffany Flowers, the healthy nut and OMG! (Oh Mama Green)

Karen Weigert, Mayor Rahm Emanuel's Chief Sustainability Officer

Erika Allen, the urban farming mentor

Maria Lawrence, the green educator

Dr. Raed Elaydi

Patrick Sablan Photography

Roosevelt University, Growing Power Chicago, and Chicago Gateway Green

Thank you little Ghabiters:

South Loop School Students, Saniya Jain, Yousef Abueida, Layla Flowers, Ayo Allen, Omar and Adon Hallab

I am especially grateful to my parents, Neeta and Arunkumar Jain, and all those who have inspired me to follow my dreams.

GHABY'S ORGANIC GARDEN

Copyright © 2013 by Ghabit LLC.

All rights reserved. No part of this book may be used or reproduced in any manner whatsoever without written permission except in the case of brief quotations embodied in critical articles and reviews.

For information regarding permission, please write to:
Permissions Department, Ghabit LLC, 1808 S. Michigan Ave., Ste. 34, Chicago, IL 60616

Ghabit, Ghaby and associated logos are trademarks and/or registered trademarks of Ghabit LLC.

Eco-Printed in the United States of America on FSC certified 100% Recycled Paper, Chlorine free processing, Non-toxic ink for safe handling by children, and De-inkable printing allows for easy recycling.

www.ghabit.com

Library of Congress Control Number: 2013936852   ISBN: 978-0-9891604-1-4

What is organic gardening?

Using healthy seeds to plant a garden.

Pete, age 6

Using earthworm poo & leftover food scraps as compost to feed the soil.

Saniya, age 9

Saying no to harmful fertilizers but planting lavender, garlic, catnip or marigold in the garden to keep the pests away.

Hal, age 8

Mary, age 7

Keeping Momma Earth happy.
When Momma Earth is happy, she provides us with healthy fruits and veggies. When I eat healthy food, I grow tall and strong.

"Eating junk food puts me in a bad mood!
Ghaby, Ghaby, what should I do?"
cried Milu.

Gwell, Gwell, Gwell!

Ghaby giggles and wiggles and starts singing...

> Healthy food is good for you,
> I told you so.
> Junk food is bad for you,
> now you know!
> Organic gardening is so easy.
> Let's grow veggies— it's a breezy!
>
> All it takes is 10 Ghabit habits
> that I learned from planet Ghabit!
> Off we go, off we go.
> Put on your boots; grab your shovel.
> Off we go!

Ghabit Habit #1

Find a spot in the sun,
to dig a hole one by one.

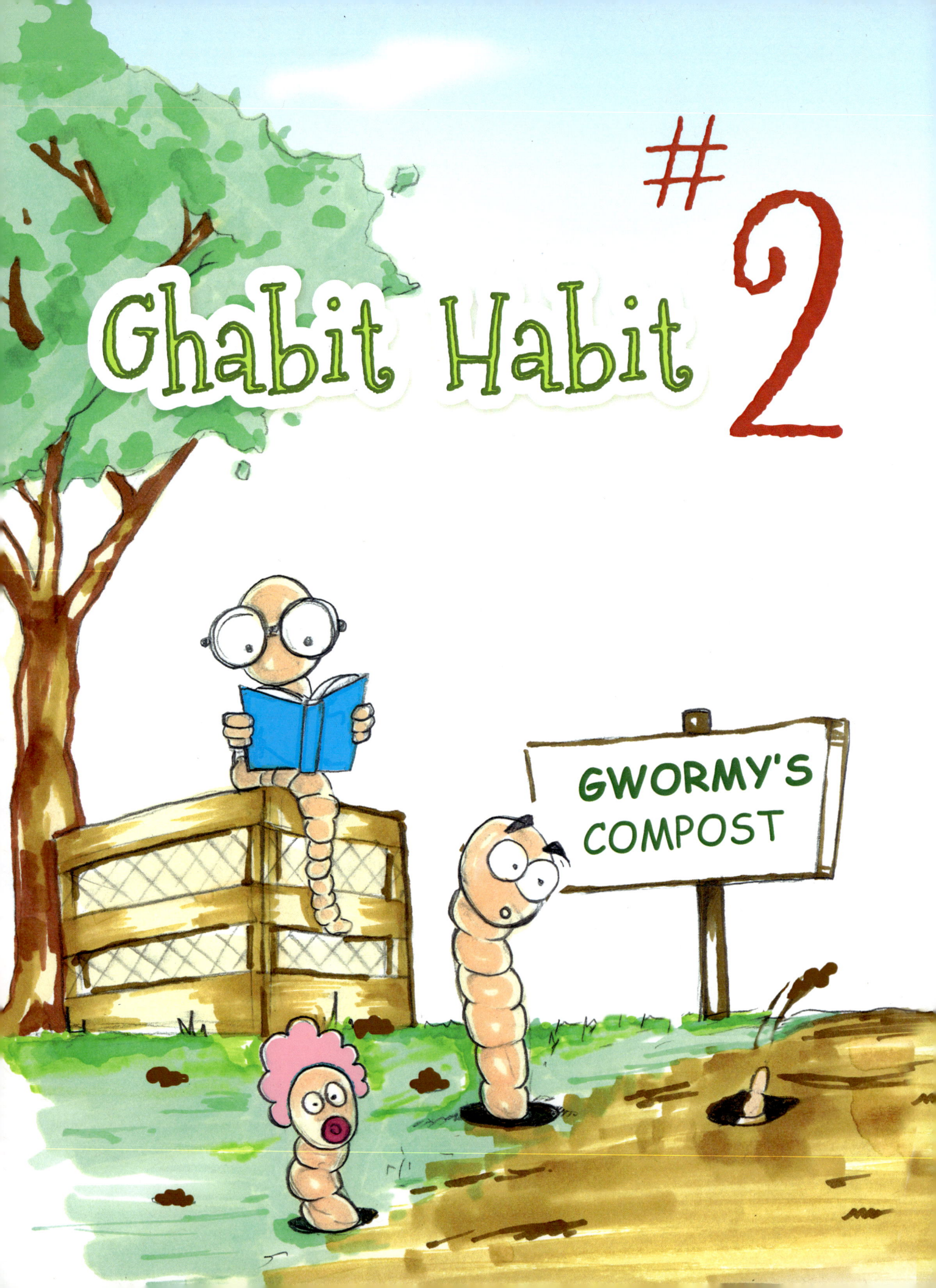

Let the earthworms
go poo-poo
to nourish the soil
two by two.

Ghabit Habit #3

Make the pesky pests flee flee flee,
by planting lavender, garlic and catnip,
three by three.

Ghabit Habit #4

Be nice!

Ask the bees for the seeds they've stored,

then scatter the lovey seeds,

four by four.

Ghabit Habit #5

Water the plants so they'll thrive.
Sprinkle drops five by five.

Ghabit Habit #6

Keep the garden in happy mix,
by pulling weeds six by six.

Ghabit Habit #7

Tell the plants to breathe air from our blue sky haven, and they'll grow as tall as giants! Seven by seven.

Ghabit Habit #8

Be patient!
Now just you wait,
veggies ripen eight by eight.

Ghabit Habit #9

Pick the veggies off the vine,
time to dine, nine by nine.

Ghabit Habit #10

Plant organic gardens, again and again, healthy habits ten by ten.

"Organic food is the way to go!
My tummy tells me this is so.
Eating healthy helps me grow!
I am happy from head to toe!"

Thank you Momma Earth, for your care. We promise to plant organic gardens everywhere!

Ghabit
make green a habit

Author's Note:

When I was a little boy, I used to love drawing penguins and coloring them green. You see, green was my favorite color. In fact, I was in the green group in my school. My green penguin's name was Ghaby, and we were best friends.

We used to sit by the windowsill watching the blue waters of the Arabian sea, imagining a faraway land where everything was green. It was a magical place where everything came to life. Yes, even Ghaby would start singing and dancing!

We would slide through the hills, sing with the birds and eat fresh fruits and honey from my green paradise. On one of our adventures, I saved a glow earthworm, from choking on an apple seed. It sounds silly, but our dreams matter!

And here I am years later, using Ghaby to educate others so those dreams of a greener world can become reality! The books and products of Ghabit are here to help others learn about honoring our planet and developing greener habits.

Working together we can each leave a greener footprint on this earth.

Green at heart,

Milesh Jain
aka Dr. Ghabit